Self-Feeders

A Personal and Corporate Key to Lasting Fruit
in the Christian Life

Todd Doxzon

sermontobook
.com

Sermon To Book
www.sermontobook.com

Self-Feeders / Todd Doxzon
ISBN-13: 978-1-952602-05-4

This book is dedicated to my wife, Denise, and our twin boys, Tzion and Blaze. It's such a blast doing life with you!

Denise—you are, hands down, the most beautiful (inside and out), selfless, thoughtful woman in the world. Your passion and love for Jesus and His people are astounding.

Tzion—you are a brilliant, steady, handsome dude who will change the world.

Blaze—you are a disciplined, hardworking, chiseled beast who will be a game changer wherever God takes you.

I can't believe how blessed I am that God gave you guys to me!

I also want to dedicate this book to all the amazing staff and volunteers at Love Church. What an honor and privilege to serve alongside such a genuine, loving, supportive, "all in" family!

In powerful yet succinct ways, Todd encourages us all to become men and women who are filled up and nourished by the Bible. The impact of a daily diet of the Word is profound, and Todd delivers that message uniquely and poignantly in *Self-Feeders*.

Ben Malcolmson—right-hand man to Seattle Seahawks coach Pete Carroll and author of *Walk On*

Todd knows well that there's no success without a successor. In this book he is a Moses to your Joshua, an Elijah to your Elisha, and a Paul to your Titus, mentoring you one-on-one. In *Self-Feeders*, Todd serves you a heavy dose of encouragement nourishment. In imitation of Jesus at the Last Supper, Todd offers you a meal. Jesus, the bread of heaven, was born in a feeding trough in Bethlehem (house of bread)—also nicknamed Ephratha (fruit bearing)—because He offered His body as bread and brought to bear His blood as the fruit of the vine. So, too, Todd pours himself out for us in this book. He has sacrificed much fleshing out the ideas found in *Self-Feeders*. Once you reach the final pages, you will feel empowered and ennobled to do what others won't do today so you can have what others can't have tomorrow. Come to the feast, and you'll be spiritually glutted by this most sumptuous fare!

Ben Courson—Pastor of Hope Generation

The paradox of the Christian life is that in every step forward toward maturity and growth, you never get to move on from the basics. Todd's practical tools and wisdom in this book will teach you that reading God's Word will never get old if you keep asking Him to show you something new. I truly believe it will propel you forward in your walk with Christ.

Levi Lusko—Lead Pastor of Fresh Life Church and best-selling author

Research is clear—the single most powerful habit for transforming your walk with Jesus is reading your Bible every day. Todd and Denise have modeled this discipline and seen habit turn to delight. I pray this book inspires you to do the same.

Doug Sauder—Lead Pastor of Calvary Chapel Fort Lauderdale

CONTENTS

A Daily Diet of God's Word

The apostle Paul wrote, "How terrible for me if I didn't preach the Good News!" (1 Corinthians 9:16). Well, if I were writing a book of the Bible—1 Doxzonians—I would write, "How terrible for me if I don't teach people to grow in their knowledge of God through reading the Bible daily on their own!"

I'm called to give my life to this mission, and that is the main point of this book. I hope to convince and empower you to have a daily diet of God's Word so you can experience all that God has for you.

Many give their lives to Christ, but few mature and bear fruit that lasts throughout their lifetime. Many people start churches and ministries, but few last for a lifetime and make disciples who also make disciples, even when things get tough. Few finish well.

What makes the difference between those who limp through their Christian life and those who bear fruit and finish well? What is the key to longevity? I am convinced that it is a daily diet of God's Word.

When I was playing professional football, I had a daily workout regimen. If I went more than a few days without training, I felt it on the field. The same thing can happen if you aren't reading your Bible regularly. Too many Christians are trying to go out and take on the world with little or no Word in them. That leads to firework Christians, believers who are loud in their salvation and beautiful in their testimony but sputter out almost immediately. Jesus compared them to sprouts planted in shallow soil that quickly wilt and wither (Matthew 13:5–6).

If you aren't interested in "flash in the pan" Christianity or ministry, then this book is for you. If you're tired of seeing your own walk falter and the people you lead sputter, then this book is for you. To be honest, I'm tired of one-and-dones. The stakes are too high for us to go back to the vomit of our past (Proverbs 26:11).

All of us go through ups and downs. My life has been no different. However, if someone were to ask me to pinpoint one thing that has been the key to me staying in the game and not wandering in my faith, I would say that it is *daily Bible study*. This has been my anchor through all the changes in my life.

Since I first read the Bible from cover to cover in 2001, I have moved twenty-three times, played for eight professional football teams, had multiple injuries, attended Bible college, and started a church. However, daily feasting on the Word has been my solid foundation. Through all the changes, one thing has remained constant: daily time in the Word of God, staying close to Jesus, getting to know Him deeper and deeper every day.

I want this for you, too, for every Christian. This book discusses three key areas that will help you to develop the discipline of the daily study of God's Word:

- Desire

- Diligence

- Abiding

At the end of each chapter, I have provided workbook sections that include reflective questions and action steps both for individual believers and for church leaders.

A daily diet of God's Word is vital for experiencing the fullest life possible in Christ. My prayer is that this book will help you to develop the discipline and give you the tools to make Bible reading a habit in your own life. Ask God to open your heart and give you courage to make the necessary changes that will help you to bear fruit in your Christian life and ministries through a daily diet of God's living Word.

CHAPTER ONE

Desiring God's Word Daily

Early in my adult life, I thought I knew where I was going and where God was taking me. I was newly married and had begun a great career as a professional football player. Life was good!

What I didn't know was that God had something completely different planned, and He was going to use a preaching elder at a church we visited to change the course of my life. When you make a real commitment to follow the Lord, expect real change!

A Pro Football Player
Becomes a Daily Bible Reader

When I pulled up to our townhouse in Pompano Beach, Florida, in August of 2000, my stomach churned with dread. I had been married for just three months, and we were still in the honeymoon stage. Life was rosy and exciting. I had been living my dream as a football player. We were madly in love, and we were stoked about the upcoming season. However, my entire world was now crashing down around me.

Just a few hours earlier, my coach, Dave Wandstat, called me into his office to inform me that I would no longer be employed by the Miami Dolphins. He had hired Chan Gailey, the former Dallas Cowboys head coach, as his offensive coordinator. Coach Gailey wanted to bring on a guy from the Cowboys whom he really liked, a player named Jeff Ogden. Ogden was a similar player to me, a slot receiver and punt returner.

So, instead of giving me a chance to make the team in camp, they decided to cut me before it even started. Ogden had proven himself already to the new coach, and I was suddenly expendable. My job as a professional football player seemed to be over. Pulling into our driveway that day, I knew that I would have to break the bad news to my bride, and our lives would change drastically.

My wife, Denise, took the news like a champ, and we committed to praying for God to direct our next steps. For the next couple of months, I worked for a demo crew. We demoed houses, which was a great way to take out frustration! One Sunday in October, I was watching my former team, the Dolphins, play on TV, and I was heartbroken. I paused and prayed to God, telling Him that I was fine being done with playing football if that's what He wanted. "But please, Lord, direct me now to what's next!"

The very next day, I got a call from Al Luginbill, who had just gotten the head coaching job for the Los Angeles Extreme of the newly formed league called the XFL. He had been my coach in NFL Europe and wanted to see if I still wanted to pursue football since the XFL draft was coming up soon. Talk about a quick answer to prayer! He picked me in the seventh round of the draft, and I was officially on the roster for the team. Training camp would start in January 2001 in Las Vegas. After a couple of months of rigorous training in Florida, Denise and I packed our bags and headed out west. Our lives were changing, but our dreams still seemed intact.

On the way to Las Vegas, my wife and I happened to stop at a Calvary Chapel church in Phoenix, Arizona, on December 31, 2000. It was a Sunday night service. The pastor wasn't there, but an elder was teaching for him that night. The elder's teaching was all about the importance of daily Bible study. He guaranteed that our lives would change if we read through the entire Bible throughout the next year.

After the service that night, there were daily reading charts on a table for us to pick up. When I walked by, I thought, "There's no way I could read through the entire Bible in one year. Shoot, I don't even like to read! I've never liked to read." If my activities didn't have to do with throwing, catching, or shooting a ball, I wasn't interested.

The Bible was so big, so long, so confusing. It looked good on my bedside table and when I carried it to church, but what was the point of reading it myself if a pastor would tell me what it all meant anyway? I mean, how could a book that is thousands of years old have anything to do with my life in the twenty-first century? But just when I was about to pass it by, my wife nudged me with her elbow. She wanted me to grab a couple of those reading charts. Being the loving husband that I am and wanting to please her, I grudgingly picked up a couple of charts.

We arrived in Vegas a few days later, and I started training camp, which was about a month long. I got into the routine of practice, but the Bible reading challenge never left my thoughts. I knew that I needed to figure out a way to start it. So, here's what I did. After each practice as a receiver, I got into the "cold tub." This was a metal tub that looked like a horse trough. After I got in, they filled it with ice water and turned on a whirlpool feature that made the water swirl around. I had to wear neoprene toe cups so my toes wouldn't fall off in the frigid water. This bath helped to reduce the soreness of my legs after so much running in practice, but it was not for the faint of heart.

I had to be in the ice tub for about fifteen minutes, and I needed a distraction from my icy bath. Since fifteen minutes was about the amount of time I needed for my daily Bible reading on the program, I started reading the Bible there. For the next three weeks during training, I didn't miss a day. It was a natural way of making room in my schedule to start the habit of daily Bible reading. I didn't need a special room, absolute quiet, a seminary degree, or Billy Graham to break down the Hebrew or Greek. I just needed fifteen minutes, and I chose to use the fifteen minutes I spent in the cold tub.

This was the beginning of a habit that would change the course of my life. What my wife and I didn't know that night at the Calvary Chapel in Phoenix was that the elder's challenge for that coming new year would forever change my family's life. God used that Sunday night sermon and those little Bible reading charts to set the course for the church we would start eight years later—and to lead me to write this book you are reading right now.

After barely making that XFL team in Los Angeles, I tore a ligament in my knee on the very first play of the season. I then went on to play five seasons in the Arena Football League in New York, Carolina, and Georgia. Each off season, Denise and I hosted a small-group Bible study at our off-season home in Omaha, Nebraska. The group grew each week until we had to leave to start the next season. I retired from football after the 2005 season and took a job with the Fellowship of Christian Athletes in Omaha.

Our small-group home Bible study continued to grow and was turning into a small church. I got on the phone with our pastor at Calvary Chapel Fort Lauderdale and asked him for advice. He told us to move down to Fort Lauderdale, go on staff at the church, and get some solid on-the-job training for a few years. Then, he said, they would send us back to start a Calvary Chapel in Omaha.

That's exactly what we did! We sold everything, moved to Fort Lauderdale, went on staff, and learned every part of ministry on the job. After about two years, Denise and I felt called to come back to start the church in Omaha. In February 2008, we headed back to Omaha and began teaching the Bible at Kiewit Middle School on Easter 2008. Calvary Chapel West Omaha, which is now called Love Church, officially began. Through our ministry, we have seen the spiritual discipline of daily Bible reading change hundreds of lives, and we know that it can change yours, too.

Moving from Duty to Delight

I will be the first to admit that when you first start reading the Bible as a daily habit, it may feel like a duty. You may not feel particularly excited about reading the Bible, and you may not come away from your time in the Word with any amazing new insights or a spiritual high. Be patient. Over time, the habit becomes a discipline. Eventually your feelings will follow, and then Bible reading will become a delight. Duty—the obligation we feel to obey God, even when we don't yet find joy in our obedience—is sometimes a necessary step to developing a discipline that later becomes a delight.

> *Work hard so you can present yourself to God and receive his approval.*
> **—2 Timothy 2:15**

This verse from 2 Timothy is about diligence. For something that's a duty to become a delight, you need to keep working at it. God approves of diligence, and He will reward you with delight.

Considering 2 Timothy 2:15, can you think of anything you have had to work at diligently that eventually became a delight in your life? What are you good at doing? What do you do consistently? What are you diligent about doing? You may love sports, as I do, so you know that hard, daily, consistent work is required to become a successful athlete. You may be great in academics, but you know that you can't just show up and take tests. You must read the books, do the homework, write the papers, and attend each class. If you are into the arts, whether visual or performing, you know that you need training, practice, and consistent work at your craft to get and stay good at it.

The Greek word translated as "work hard" in 2 Timothy 2:15 is *spoudazo*, which means to exert oneself.[1] Why would you think that the discipline of Bible reading is any different? A daily Bible reading habit doesn't just happen; it takes concentrated effort.

When I started reading my Bible daily during my cold-tub time at training camp in Vegas, it felt like drudgery. I told myself, "Okay. I *have* to do this." It wasn't always easy or fun. But after that month in camp, it turned into a daily discipline. I barely made the team that year, but I, along with my wife, continued that Bible-in-a-year plan. We realized that when we read the Bible every day, we were getting to know God in ways that were blowing our minds. It was only a few months later that I had so developed an appetite for God's Word that I began delighting to get into God's Word, to dine with Him, to share an intimate meal with my Savior.

It didn't end there. After reading through the Bible in 2001, we started again in 2002. We completed it again the next several years. In fact, my wife is currently reading through the Bible in a year for her twentieth time. I've since changed it up. I switched to a two-year plan in 2011, which forced me to go a little more slowly through each book. In 2014, I started a Bible-in-six-years plan that covers the Pentateuch in the first year, the historical books in the second year, poetic and wisdom literature in the third year, the prophets in the fourth year, the Gospels and Acts in the fifth year, and the epistles in the sixth year. Most recently, in 2019, I read through the Gospels and Acts and have encouraged our church to do so as well.

Something that started as a way to pass the time in the cold tub became a daily habit that I now look forward to doing. It was a process, but by God's grace, it happened.

Start Small—Start Today!

If you desire to grow as a Christian, both in your personal life and any ministry God has called you to, you must desire to drink from God's Word daily. Jesus said, "I am the bread of life. Whoever comes to me will never be hungry again. Whoever believes in me will never be thirsty" (John 6:35). To get that bread of life, you need to be in the Word.

In 1 Corinthians 3:2, the apostle Paul likened gradual Bible learning to a baby starting out with milk and eventually being able to eat solid food. As you grow in the Word, you will begin to eat more solid food—that is, you will be able to handle deeper teaching. However, it's a process, and it takes time. When you first begin a daily Bible reading habit, think of it as starting with milk and purees and working up to meat. Be patient with yourself.

You must start somewhere, though, so I have a challenge for you. Read the Bible every time you eat a meal. Develop a habit of only eating physical food if you couple it with spiritual food. This isn't a biblical command, but since you must sit and eat at some point in the day, why not pair it with Bible reading? It's a natural way, just like my cold-tub bath was, to start a daily Bible reading habit. Every time you eat some grub, crack open your Bible and ask God to speak to you.

Maybe grab a pen or highlighter, think about what you read throughout the day, and see if this habit starts to change anything in your life. I guarantee that it will! We have a saying we use around the church: "Whoever you feed is going to lead." Feed yourself with healthy spiritual food, and odds are that the Spirit will lead your life. Fruit will include "love, joy, peace, patience, kindness, goodness, faithfulness, gentleness, and self-control" (Galatians 5:22–23).

In the following chapters, we will explore in greater depth why Bible reading is so vital, including the dangers to your spiritual life if you avoid it, as well as why you need to do it yourself instead of just listening to pastors and teachers who do it for you. We will also look at some good methods for studying the Bible yourself.

I encourage you to take this moment, right now, to accept the challenge of beginning your daily Bible reading habit today. You won't regret it!

WORKBOOK

Chapter One Questions

Question: Describe your own habits when it comes to reading God's Word. Have you ever read through the entire Bible? How frequently do you read Scripture? What other forms of Bible "intake"—such as audio recordings, in-depth Bible studies, or Scripture memory plans—are part of your life?

_____

_____

_____

_____

_____

_____

_____

_____

_____

Question: Where have commitment and discipline paid off in other areas of your life? What are some ways in which the Bible has already changed your life? How could consistently spending more time in the Word help you to grow in your walk with the Lord?

_____

_____

_____

_____

_____

_____

_____

_____

_____

_____

_____

Action: Write out your commitment to spend time in God's Word each day. Begin thinking through logistical questions, such as what time of day works best for you, whether you will read a physical Bible or an app, and which translation (version) you will use.

For Church Leaders

Question: In what ways do you challenge your church members to be in God's Word? Do you provide tools and encouragement to help them develop and maintain this habit?

_____

_____

_____

_____

_____

_____

_____

_____

_____

_____

_____

Question: Are your own devotional habits to a point where you could invite the church to follow your example when it comes to Bible reading and study? Where do you need to improve personally to practice what you preach?

_____

_____

_____

_____

_____

_____

_____

_____

_____

_____

_____

Action: Begin planning now for a special-emphasis Sunday when you invite your congregation to join you in a specific Bible reading challenge. Research various Bible reading plans and, if possible, purchase a tool—such as reading-plan pamphlets, an app or software, or physical Bibles designed to be read through in a year—to inspire your members and help them to stay faithful to the specific challenge you present.

There are many sources of excellent Bible reading plans. For example, Life Church has many good reading plans on the Bible app. We at Love Church also have plans we'd be happy to give you if you reach out to us. Tyndale makes custom chronological *One Year Bibles* that you can take your church through.

Chapter One Notes

_____

_____

_____

_____

_____

_____

_____

_____

_____

_____

_____

_____

_____

_____

_____

_____

_____

_____

_____

_____

_____

CHAPTER TWO

It's a Matter of Life and Death

It's not an accident that Jesus referred to Himself as "the bread of life" (John 6:35). This concept isn't unique to the New Testament. God wanted to be the Israelite's source of sustenance in the Old Testament, too.

The Word of God as Manna

Exodus tells the story of the Jews as they escaped bondage in Egypt to wander the desert for forty years. Through a great miracle, they were led to safety through the parting of the Red Sea by Moses and ended up in the wilderness.

Imagine this huge group of people who just escaped slavery and had no food or water. They complained to Moses. God responded to their need and said, "I will feed you." So, in Exodus 16, God rained bread from heaven.

This is how it worked. Every morning, there was dew on the ground. It crystallized into a wafer called *manna*, which means "What is it?" (Exodus 16:15). Every day the Israelites went out in the morning to collect the bread they needed for the day. It's a perfect picture and foreshadowing of our daily need for intimacy with God, just like we need food every day.

Notice that Exodus 16:4 specifies that the people were to gather their own bread. Moses wasn't going to do it for them. They were responsible for their own sustenance. Just like the Israelites were not to rely on Moses for their food, you and I are not to rely solely on Bible teachers for our biblical nourishment. God expects us to do it ourselves, to become self-feeders!

Are You Surviving on Baby Food?

Jesus said that He is "the bread of life" (John 6:35). He wants you to dine with Him daily and listen to Him. He is the Word that allows you to connect with Him and grow deeper in your relationship with God. Through daily Bible reading, the Holy Spirit gives you the tools to live a life that honors Him.

What if, as an adult, you only ate one jar of baby food once a week on Sunday? You would starve. Like a baby, you wouldn't be chewing your food (working to understand the Bible). You wouldn't be getting any home-cooked meals (studying the Bible for yourself). When you rely on a once-a-week sermon to get you through the week spiritually and never dust off your Bible between Sundays, it's really just not enough to grow and mature.

When I'm getting ready to preach the Word of God, I spend a lot of time preparing the message by consuming the Word of God. I'm getting a rich, meaty meal, but if you are counting on just my teachings to get you through the week, you're essentially surviving on one jar of pureed carrots per week.

I call this spiritual anorexia. You become frail. You have no strength. You lose your power to fight the normal struggles of life and deal with sin. You need to be reading the Bible for yourself to get the proper spiritual nutrition to live a victorious life that glorifies God.

Reasons You May Avoid Personal Bible Study

I have heard lots of different reasons people have for not reading the Bible regularly, and truthfully, I used to make all the same excuses myself. Let's look at some of them.

1. The Bible is big, old, and overwhelming. The Bible consists of sixty-six books written by multiple authors from multiple walks of life. It was written over a period of several thousand years. It is ancient. It was not originally written in English but was translated from Ancient Hebrew, Ancient Greek, and Aramaic, a language that doesn't even exist anymore. Some of those Bible books, especially in the Old Testament, consist of long lists of names that we can't pronounce. Those facts alone make Bible reading an intimidating prospect for many.

2. You don't understand the biblical culture. The cultures of ancient Israel, the Middle East, and the ancient Roman empire are far removed from our modern American culture. Some things that happened in the Bible just seem weird because you don't understand the cultural context. This is another reason why you may avoid reading the Bible. It may seem like too much work to figure all of that out.

3. You feel like you have the big questions already figured out. If you have been a Christian for a long time, you may think that you've got this Jesus thing down. You know the basics of the gospel and the main rules of Christian living, and you think you're set. You think that you don't need to read the Bible because you know it all already.

4. You don't have time. Most of us start our Christian walks with a lot of enthusiasm. However, once that initial spiritual high of salvation is over, we get into our life routines. We have careers. We're building families. We get busy with our kids and our hobbies. Bible reading just seems to be one more thing we must add to our already long to-do lists. Other things often seem much more urgent, so daily time in God's Word gets squeezed out.

The Dangers of Being Deprived of God's Word

One thing I have observed throughout my years in ministry is that the busyness of life and its distractions end up sucking many people's attention away from the Lord, even if they started out following Jesus enthusiastically. Instead of maturing in their faith over time, they either give up on loving and seeking Jesus in any meaningful way or, at best, remain immature Christians. Never growing up in the faith, the immature live on the spiritual equivalent of milk and pureed carrots their whole lives.

In the Parable of the Sower, Jesus explained that the seed that fell on rocky soil "represents those who hear the message and immediately receive it with joy. But since they don't have deep roots, they don't last long. They fall away as soon as they have problems or are persecuted for believing God's word" (Matthew 13:20–21). If you don't spend time in God's Word every day, studying it for yourself and applying it to your specific life situations, then you risk becoming the seed that fell on rocky soil.

When you are deprived of God's Word, your spirit is weak, just as your physical body would be weak without food. You don't have the power or authority to change your life in the way you would with daily time in the Word. The Bible says, "My people are being destroyed because they don't know me" (Hosea 4:6). Notice that it doesn't say you die because you don't wear the right outfit to church or you sing off-key or you sit in someone's seat. These are human problems. What God tells us is that not *knowing* Him can cause spiritual death.

What would happen if you didn't eat for weeks at a time? Unfortunately, spiritual anorexia is a real thing. The tragic truth is that there are many malnourished, stagnant spiritual infants in the church today because of believers not developing a daily diet of God's Word.

We stop thinking that reading the Bible daily for ourselves is important, and then we wonder why the body of Christ in America is ineffective! Even worse, we start seeing the effects this spiritual immaturity has on society in general. When we are weak in our relationship with God, we lose our ability to share the gospel and change our culture for the better.

We are at a critical season in the history of our country. What started as a country founded upon the principles and tenants of the Word of God has slowly but surely eroded into a country where everyone does what's right in his or her own eyes (Judges 17:6). Instead of having a strong compass or playbook to guide us and a solid foundation to ground us, we have lost our way and do whatever we want.

The results of this are tragic. Our national debt exceeds $20 trillion and continues climbing.[2] Since abortion became legalized in 1970, more than sixty million babies have been murdered.[3] Violence is escalating, and so is perversity. Revenue for pornography is more than the NFL, MLB, and NBA combined.[4] When Christians don't make reading the Bible a priority, we lose our saltiness and our ability to be lights in a world that so desperately needs the gospel (Matthew 5:13–16).

The same thing happened in ancient Israel. After Moses died, Joshua was appointed in his place as leader and brought the Israelites to the promised land. God drove out their enemies and told them to worship Him alone. But over time, they adopted their enemies' way of life and worship. They turned from the Lord to other gods.

Second Chronicles 33 recounts the story of Manasseh. Under his rule, the Israelites reached new lows of evil. The Bible says that Manasseh "murdered many innocent people until Jerusalem was filled from one end to the other with innocent blood" (2 Kings 21:16). Perversity abounded, and Manasseh himself sacrificed his children as burnt offerings to false gods. All of this happened because the people of Israel turned from worshiping the Lord to acting as they saw fit.

They were headed toward destruction, but God raised up King Josiah. Second Chronicles 34 and 35 tell his amazing story. He became king at eight years of age, and by the time he was twenty, he was already destroying the pagan shrines and purifying Judah of its idols. He invested money to repair Solomon's dilapidated temple. During its renovation, one of the priests found scrolls containing the Book of the Law, God's law. This information was brought to Josiah, who read the entire book aloud in the temple. Before the people, he renewed the nation's commitment to the Lord and promised to obey God's commands.

Josiah's thirty-one-year reign was characterized by a rebirth of commitment to the Lord and His Word. When you do the same thing in your life, when you commit to studying God's Word for yourself and applying it to your life, you will see similar renewal and rebirth.

Are You a Self-Feeder?

A self-feeder is someone who reads the Bible for him- or herself. Many Christians have somehow come to believe that only pastors and professionals should read the Bible every day. The rest of us just show up to hear what people we consider to be experts say about the Bible. We take their word for it instead of getting to know God for ourselves one day at a time. Self-feeders no longer rely only on what pastors or their grandmothers say. They study the Bible daily to hear what God Himself says.

If you are a Christian and don't read the Bible, that's

like saying you're married but not really listening to or hanging out with your spouse. Or if you do, it's for thirty minutes a week. You could also liken it to having a best friend you never spend time with or communicate with, except for a thirty-minute texting session each week.

How do you think those relationships would work out? They wouldn't be very deep, and both people would feel disconnected and even short-changed. Those relationships would be under a lot of strain and would be difficult to maintain. A marriage like that would be a farce at best. We do the exact same thing with God when we don't spend time with Him in the Word, yet we wonder why we feel disconnected from Him and why our lives are void of His power.

At this point, you may feel like I've sent you on a long-winded guilt trip. Please know that's not my goal! I'm not saying this to shame you at all. I say this because I want what's best for you. I want you to be strong and healthy. I want your relationship with God to be strong and healthy. I want your relationships with your spouse and your kids to be strong and healthy. If you start the habit of self-feeding on God's Word, you will be powerfully equipped every single day to live the life God has called you to live.

I've spent a lot of time talking about all of the problems that come from not having a daily diet of God's Word, and you've had a chance to examine your heart and be honest about where you are with this. So, where do we go from here? In the next chapter, I'll discuss all the benefits of feasting on God's Word, and I'll give you the tools you need to start this habit successfully in your own life.

Chapter Two Questions

Question: Look at the list of reasons people avoid personal Bible study. Have you ever used one of these excuses? Can you think of other excuses that have kept you from the Word?

_____

_____

_____

_____

_____

_____

_____

_____

_____

_____

Question: Do you tend to look first to the Bible or to Christian teachers, preachers, celebrities, and experts to tell you what God thinks about a certain topic or situation? What Bible verses offer reassurance that you, as a believer, can understand and learn directly from the Bible without needing an intermediary? Read 1 Timothy 2:5 and Acts 4:13 to get started. To what standards should you hold any preacher or teacher, no matter how well-respected he or she is, before you receive wisdom or advice from that person?

_____

_____

_____

_____

_____

_____

_____

_____

_____

_____

_____

Action: Write out and memorize the following verses about the importance of God's Word and the power of its influence in your life: 2 Timothy 3:14–17, Hebrews 4:12, Psalm 119:9–16, and John 17:17.

For Church Leaders

Question: When people ask you what God thinks about a certain topic or situation, do you simply offer them your personal opinion or teaching, or do you point them back to the Word of God and encourage them to seek an answer for themselves? Why is it sometimes hard for pastors and other leaders to encourage personal Bible study over formulated answers from supposed experts?

_____

_____

_____

_____

_____

_____

_____

_____

_____

_____

_____

_____

Question: Describe some of the specific effects of biblical illiteracy you see in the church, the culture, and the nation. How can you and your church promote greater understanding of and appreciation for the Bible, beginning within your church and also reaching out into your community and beyond?

_____

_____

_____

_____

_____

_____

_____

_____

_____

_____

_____

_____

_____

Action: Research the influence (or lack thereof) of the Bible in your community. Are there parachurch groups with which you could partner (e.g. the Gideons or Good News Clubs)? What are the legal and/or business requirements to distribute or display Scriptures in public places? What opinions do people in your community have of the Bible? Consider organizing your own survey and seeing how your community's attitudes line up with national research by groups such as Barna Group.

Chapter Two Notes

_____

_____

_____

_____

_____

_____

_____

_____

_____

_____

_____

_____

_____

_____

_____

_____

_____

_____

_____

_____

_____

_____

CHAPTER THREE

Abiding in God's Word Daily

A habit of daily Bible reading will produce lasting fruit in your Christian life. It is imperative that we self-feed on the Word of God.

> *Like newborn babies, you must crave pure spiritual milk so that you will grow into a full experience of salvation. Cry out for this nourishment, now that you have had a taste of the Lord's kindness.*
> **—1 Peter 2:2–3**

This verse reveals that we are to desire the pure milk of the Word so that we will grow from it, like infants grow from their early nourishment.

My wife and I have twin boys, Tzion and Blaze. They are eighteen years old now. Just hours after my wife, Denise, gave birth, the doctors' main concern was that the boys develop an appetite. Denise was trying to feed Blaze, who was only four pounds, six ounces. I had Tzion, who was a little bigger. I remember putting that tiny bottle in Tzion's mouth and praying that he would drink. I wanted him to survive and grow.

Blaze, the smaller one, could barely breathe and didn't want to eat at first. But over the next couple of days, he developed an appetite. He was always ready to eat when Mom was ready to feed him. When he got older and it was time for rice cereal, he downed that. Just the other day, I took him to out to eat, and he crushed a double cheeseburger in thirty seconds!

This is a perfect picture of Peter's heart command here: that Christians would desire the pure milk of the Word, then move from milk to meat. We can do this only if we commit to self-feeding on the Word of God on a consistent, daily basis.

Your Diet Determines Your Destiny

Just as you can become undisciplined in your eating habits and fill up on pizza, chips, and cookies, you can also consume the equivalent of mental, emotional, and spiritual junk food with how you spend your time. And just like a diet of junk food leads to health and weight problems, a spiritual diet of junk food leads to spiritual problems.

What are you consuming that affects your spiritual health, whether negatively or positively? What type of content do you take in? Video games, social media, television, and the internet all have their place, but if you are playing explicit video games, watching violent TV shows, and downloading porn off the internet, it's going to have a devastating effect on your walk with the Lord. The old adage proves true: garbage in, garbage out.

From the Devil's Diet to a Divine Diet

Your goal as a Christian should be to move from loving and consuming worldly things to loving and consuming the things of God.

Don't copy the behavior and customs of this world, but let God transform you into a new person by changing the way you think. Then you will learn to know God's will for you, which is good and pleasing and perfect.

—Romans 12:2

The less you consume of the devil's diet, meaning media and content that glorify sin, and the more you consume of a divine diet of God's Word, the better your spiritual health will be.

Many Christians today seem content with understanding the basics: salvation, general morality, and knowing the Sunday-school Bible stories of Adam and Eve, Noah, and Moses. This is what many of the writers of the New Testament's letters called "milk." There is nothing wrong with these things; in fact, they are absolutely necessary to the Christian walk and are relevant to your entire life. But if you stop there, if you don't learn to apply these truths—what the apostles Paul and Peter called "meat"—then you remain spiritually undernourished and can be easily corrupted by the sin of the world.

Moreover, some Christians read the Bible regularly, but they get stuck reading only Psalms, Proverbs, and maybe the four Gospels.

All Scripture is inspired by God and is useful to teach us what is true and to make us realize what is wrong in our lives. It corrects us when we are wrong and teaches us to do what is right. God uses it to prepare and equip his people to do every good work.

—2 Timothy 3:16–17

Did you see the word "all" at the beginning of that passage? It means that every word, sentence, chapter, and book of the Bible is meant to help you grow spiritually. If you don't spend time studying the Word and praying over it, you will miss out on truths for your life that God wants you to know and put into practice. This divine diet will change your entire life if you are willing to make the commitment to self-feed on God's Word.

The Holy Spirit Versus the Flesh

As I touched on in Chapter Two, one of the major outcomes of a life dedicated to the daily study of God's Word is that you will experience the Holy Spirit's work in your life. When the Holy Spirit is working in your life, you will be tempted to sin less often, have more victory over sin, and develop the fruit of the Spirit. Paul exhorted:

> *So I say, let the Holy Spirit guide your lives. Then you won't be doing what your sinful nature craves. ... When you follow the desires of your sinful nature, the results are very clear: sexual immorality, impurity, lustful pleasures, idolatry, sorcery, hostility, quarreling, jealousy, outbursts of anger, selfish ambition, dissension, division, envy, drunkenness, wild parties, and other sins like these. ... But the Holy Spirit produces this kind of fruit in our lives: love, joy, peace, patience, kindness, goodness, faithfulness, gentleness, and self-control.*
> **—Galatians 5:16, 19–21, 22–23**

Spiritually starved Christians struggle more with sin. Christians who feast on God's Word find wisdom and win the battles against temptation. The main way you can invite the Holy Spirit to do His work in your life is to study God's Word daily and allow the Holy Spirit to produce these fruits. When you do this, you'll resist the cravings of your sinful nature and find sustenance for every area of your life.

You Need Spiritual Food to Follow Jesus

Jesus said, "I tell you the truth, Moses didn't give you bread from heaven. My Father did. And now he offers you the true bread from heaven. The true bread of God is the one who comes down from heaven and gives life to the world."
—John 6:32–33

Jesus was referencing the Exodus miracle of manna (Exodus 16), and when He talked about the bread from heaven, He was talking about Himself.

"Sir," they said, "give us that bread every day."

Jesus replied, "I am the bread of life. Whoever comes to me will never be hungry again. Whoever believes in me will never be thirsty."
—John 6:34–35

When you abide with Jesus daily by studying His Word, praying, and following His commands, He becomes your satisfaction. Just as the Israelites had to go out every day and gather the manna they would eat, you have to return to Scripture daily to gather fuel and spiritual food. What you glean from the Word is enough only for that day. You need to return to the Word every day to grow spiritually and grow closer to God.

One of my main passions is to see people become self-feeders on the Word of God. It drives the ministry I am a part of. The main reason we planted our church was because we wanted to reach lost people and help Christians to become self-feeders. It's also the reason I'm writing this book.

If I can help you to get into your own Bible and learn what God says about Himself and who He is, I know that you will grow closer to God every single day and there will be lasting fruit in your life. I want you to live God's best for your life as you get to know Him.

Christians who isolate themselves from fellowship with their church and time in the Word become easy pickings for the enemy, who comes in "like a roaring lion, looking for someone to devour" (1 Peter 5:8). Believe me, he'll pick off the weak Christians first, the ones who don't have a solid personal foundation in the Word. So, it is crucial that you develop this habit of self-feeding. Let's look at some practical ways you can do that.

Make It a Family Affair

One way to start a self-feeding habit is to get the whole family involved. Most families are busy, sometimes with both parents working, kids of different ages at different schools, and multiple sports and extracurricular activities each week to fill the schedule. However, if you want to take this self-feeding habit seriously, you may need to evaluate how your family is spending time. You may even need to cut out an activity or two to ensure that the entire family is together on a regular basis. Following God's best for your life is not always easy, and it can require sacrifices, but it's worth it.

Pick a time when your whole family will be together. Maybe you all wake up at the same time and eat breakfast together. Maybe you have consistent family dinners at home. Maybe you're at home at roughly the same time every evening and could commit to a time before bed. At Love Church, we challenge parents to read *The One Year Bible for Kids Challenge Edition* with their children every night. Whatever time you choose, make it consistent and make it an expectation that your kids and your spouse will prioritize your time in the Word together.

For many years in our home, on weekdays, anyone

under our roof (guests included) was expected downstairs in the living room at 6:30 a.m. for Bible study. We read for fifteen minutes on our own. At the end of those fifteen minutes, everyone came back to the group with something to share. We then discussed what we learned over breakfast. So, before we ate breakfast, we ate *real breakfast*. We fueled up spiritually and physically for the day.

Consuming the Word as a Personal Habit

Finding a time to study God's Word by yourself is similar to how you might go about finding a time for your family to do it together. First, think of a time each day when you know you have some downtime. Maybe you're naturally an early riser and could add it to your morning routine. Maybe you have a long commute and could listen to an audio Bible in your car. Maybe you could take your lunch hour to study while you eat. Whatever you choose, just make sure that it's consistent and that you can stick with it.

In 2004, when I played for the Georgia Force in the AFL, my time to study God's Word was in my car in the parking lot each morning before I headed into the locker room. I sang a song of worship, prayed and asked God to speak to me, and then read my "Bible in a Year" reading for that day. After about fifteen minutes, I closed that time with some prayer for my family, teammates, and coaches. I always prayed for God to open doors for me to share the gospel with my actions, my attitude, and, at times, my words.

Remember, if you're having trouble figuring out a time to do this, if you look at your life and your schedule is just too packed, start taking a hard assessment of how you're spending your time. Maybe you have twelve-hour work days and are driving your kids all over the place on the weekends, but if you have time for social media or for a

TV show in the evenings, then you have time to pray and read the Bible. You may just need to cut out some of those extra things. And remember, it's not really a sacrifice because you're trading Netflix, Instagram, or Facebook for something much more satisfying and lasting. Jesus is the bread of life!

How to Self-Feed on Scripture

Now you've picked a consistent time to study and pray, but how do you do this? There are many ways to study the Bible and countless devotionals out there to help you, but you don't really need any of that. I prefer a simple system that doesn't require an extra book with your Bible. All you need is a notebook and a pen—or, in my case, my journal Bible and a mechanical pencil.

Step 1: Pray. You should always begin your study time with prayer. The Word of God is living (Hebrews 4:12), and the Holy Spirit helps you to understand it (1 Corinthians 2:10). You'll get more out of your time if you pray to God to help you understand what you read and to teach you what He wants you to learn that day. Pray for a humble heart and the willingness to obey what you learn.

Step 2: Observe. Pick a passage to read. Don't feel like you have to read a lot at once. Sometimes a few verses is fine. Many Bibles are divided into sections with headings. These are not original to the text, but they can help to guide your reading. Read through the passage once to get the main gist. Then read through it again, this time more carefully. At this point in the study, do not try to figure out what it means. Simply observe what is in the passage.

If you're reading narrative, such as the Gospels, Acts, or the Old Testament histories, you may want to write down the who, what, when, where, why, and how. Circle any repeated words or phrases because these usually indicate something the author wanted to emphasize. Make note of anything in particular that stands out to you. Write down any questions you have. You can do this right in the Bible itself (there are even note-taking Bibles available that I use for this purpose) or separately in a journal.

Step 3: Interpret. After you've done the work of observing, it's time to figure out what the Holy Spirit is communicating through the passage. When doing this interpretation work, keep in mind that the surrounding verses, the book, the Testament, and even the whole Bible all count as context for the passage. The Bible is the best and most accurate interpreter of itself, so start there.

If you need more help with interpretation, there are many commentaries and books available. Many study Bibles have introductions and notes to help you understand the context and meaning of the passage. There are also free resources available online, like Blue Letter Bible, to help you. After I complete my daily reading each morning, I typically go to the Word for Today app and listen to what Pastor Chuck Smith has to say about the text I just read. He is the founder of the very first Calvary Chapel, and even though he is in heaven now, I still consider him my "grandpa" pastor!

The most important thing to keep in mind when interpreting the Bible is that you want to be exegetical as opposed to eisegetical. *Exegesis* is interpreting the Bible based on what it says alone, its original intent.[5] *Eisegesis* is interpreting the Bible based on reading your own philosophy, culture, or opinions into the text.[6] Eisegesis leads to misinterpretation, misunderstanding, and even heresy.

When you read the Bible and do the work of interpretation, pray against reading your own thoughts into the passage because that can corrupt the meaning. This can be very difficult to do, especially when a Bible passage seems to go against something that is culturally popular or against a deeply held belief or opinion you have. However, you must be open to allowing God's Word to challenge you and change you. That's the whole point!

Step 4: Apply. Now that you have a good grasp of the meaning of the passage, it's important that you ask yourself what God wants you—you personally and specifically—to do with that new insight. You can study the Bible until you are blue in the face, but if you don't ask God's Spirit to empower you to live it out in your own life, you won't see the blessings He has promised you.

> *But don't just listen to God's word. You must do what it says. Otherwise, you are only fooling yourselves. For if you listen to the word and don't obey, it is like glancing at your face in a mirror. You see yourself, walk away, and forget what you look like. But if you look carefully into the perfect law that sets you free, and if you do what it says and don't forget what you heard, then God will bless you for doing it.*
> *—James 1:22–25*

If you don't obey what you have read and do what it says, applying the principles to your life, changing your thinking, and working toward ending sin, then your reading is worthless. Application must be done through prayer and by the help of the Holy Spirit. Every person is different, and every situation is different. You must abide in Christ to understand how His Word applies to you specifically.

The application step highlights why it is so important to self-feed on the Word of God rather than relying on once-a-week sermons. If the only Bible you are getting every week is at church, it's easy just to sit for forty-five minutes, listen to the sermon, sing some songs, and then go about your week with your spiritual life stagnant and limp. When you read the Bible for yourself, you are forced to do the work, look at your life, and see what God wants to teach you.

Stay Strong, Steady, and Sane
by Studying Scripture

I am the true grapevine, and my Father is the gardener. He cuts off every branch of mine that doesn't produce fruit, and he prunes the branches that do bear fruit so they will produce even more. You have already been pruned and purified by the message I have given you. Remain in me, and I will remain in you. For a branch cannot produce fruit if it is severed from the vine, and you cannot be fruitful unless you remain in me.

Yes, I am the vine; you are the branches. Those who remain in me, and I in them, will produce much fruit. For apart from me you can do nothing. Anyone who does not remain in me is thrown away like a useless branch and withers. Such branches are gathered into a pile to be burned. But if you remain in me and my words remain in you, you may ask for anything you want, and it will be granted!
—John 15:1–7

The word "remain" is used seven times in this passage. We need to *remain* connected to Jesus through daily Bible reading. Proverbs 19:27 says, "If you stop listening to instruction, my child, you will turn your back on knowledge."

Have you ever worn braces on your teeth? If so, you know that you need to wear the retainer every night for the rest of your life. If you don't, your teeth will move back to their original positions. In the same way, if you don't keep up with daily Bible reading, your life will stray from God's will. The next thing you know, your life will look like a snaggle tooth!

You will never get to the end of the knowledge and blessings that God has for you in His living Word. Growing in Christ, sanctification, takes real investment, which includes committing time and energy to daily personal

Bible reading.

In this chapter, I've outlined a simple Bible study method, but there are many others available from various sources that can help you to learn from God's Word. When using a plan or devotional, however, just make sure that particular method requires exegesis of God's Word—that is, letting it speak for itself, rather than imposing your opinions or emotions onto it. Never think that the Word itself isn't sufficient for living a godly life (see 2 Peter 1:3–4). The Bible is all you need to grow in the Lord and receive all the amazing blessings He has promised you.

It's time to decide what you want in life. Whatever you are disciplined to do daily will determine your life's course. You can get caught up in the ways of the world and watch your life be ruined, or you can get caught up in intimacy with God and watch the blessings come. Abide in Him.

WORKBOOK

Chapter Three Questions

Question: What are some questions about God that you would like answered? What are some parts of the Bible you find challenging or confusing but have never taken the time to study in depth? Have you ever memorized a whole chapter of the Bible? Write out three to five goals you have for your personal Bible intake that will challenge you to get past the basics and dig deeper into God's Word than you ever have before.

_____

_____

_____

_____

_____

_____

_____

_____

_____

_____

_____

Question: What are some ways you can make Bible study a family priority? What can you do together, and how can you train your children to have their own time with the Lord? Make a list of five specific ideas that will work with the dynamics of your current household.

_____

_____

_____

_____

_____

_____

_____

_____

_____

_____

Action: For a week, carefully track how you spend your time. (Your cell phone, while often the biggest offender in wasted time, can be helpful in tracking how you are spending your time.) How are you feeding your soul? Is it all spiritual junk food and empty calories? Are you consuming the devil's diet in certain areas of your life? What plans will you put in place to balance and prioritize your time so that you are being spiritually nourished, first and foremost?

For Church Leaders

Question: If you are a teaching pastor or preacher, take inventory of your sermons. Do you preach out of the same several books of the Bible over and over, or do you present *all* Scripture to your congregation? How can you lead your church to dig deeper into some of the more challenging or more obscure parts of the Bible?

_____

_____

_____

_____

_____

_____

_____

_____

_____

_____

Question: As you teach or preach God's Word, do you make a specific call for application? How can you be more intentional in helping your congregation to apply the

Bible to their lives? How can a consistent application-oriented focus from church leaders help the congregation learn to apply their personal Bible study to their own lives?

_____

_____

_____

_____

_____

_____

_____

_____

_____

_____

_____

Action: Just as little children learn to feed themselves by watching the adults and older kids around them, so new Christians can learn to self-feed by following the example of those who already do so. Ask several mature believers who are faithful in reading and studying God's Word to train newer or less-mature believers in how to have daily time in the Word. The steps provided in this chapter will be a good starting point.

Your church can hold a special event to pair people together for this training, or it can be done in a small-group setting. After observing and learning how to spend daily time in the Word, those being discipled should commit to having their own personal time with God every day for at least a month. At Love Church, we connect people one on one for a nine-week study we call the "blue book" that helps newer believers to begin their journeys alongside a caring, loving Shepherd.

Chapter Three Notes

_____

_____

_____

_____

_____

_____

_____

_____

_____

_____

_____

_____

_____

_____

_____

_____

_____

_____

_____

_____

_____

_____

_____

_____

CONCLUSION

The Ingredients for Revival

I hope that you've come to the end of this little book not feeling guilty about all the things you're not doing, but rather empowered and motivated to get started with a rich, meaty diet of God's Word.

Revival starts in the mirror. If you want to see your family, your church, your community, and our nation changed for the better and brought back to God, you must start with yourself. You must start obeying and following God in your own life. If you want to know how to do that, you must start self-feeding on the Word of God.

Remember the story of Josiah from 2 Chronicles 34–35 that I discussed in Chapter Two of this book? Josiah followed a succession of evil, wicked kings in Judah who led the people astray, away from God. When Josiah became king as a little boy, he was different. He loved God. One of his workers, Hilkiah, found God's lost law hidden in the temple. He led the last spiritual revival of Judah before they went into captivity in Babylon in 586 B.C.[7] God's Word, empowered by the Holy Spirit, is the only thing that will start a revival in our own nation. Based on this example, I believe that there are three main ingredients for revival.

First Ingredient: Recovery

Let's be honest. The Bible is a foreign book. Many regular churchgoers don't even have one. Just like in Judah, God's Word needs to be recovered for us, His people. Have you ever lost your keys? Without your keys, you can't lock your doors, and you can't start your car. If the Bible is the key to your life, how can you expect to be a productive Christian without it?

You may be in a difficult season of life. Your life is out of control, and you're not sure what crazy new thing tomorrow is going to bring. Consider whether part of the reason you're in such a mess is that your Bible has been buried. It's under an inch of dust, and you haven't cracked it open in years. You don't even know how far you've strayed because you haven't let the Bible tell you.

Maybe you used to have regular intimate time with the Lord, but life carried you away from that, and you lost the habit. You got caught up in your work, your relationships, and your hobbies, and God's Word got pushed to the back burner. Now it's getting cold and dusty in the corner.

Whichever end of that spectrum you fall on, you need to recover God's Word. Just like Hilkiah found God's Word, seemingly forgotten, in the temple and gave it to his king, who used it to bring the Jews back to the Lord (2 Chronicles 34:14–33), you need to recover the Word in your own life.

Second Ingredient: Reading

At this point, you're probably convinced of the importance of God's Word. However, if you don't read your Bible, revival can't happen. It's like trying to make a protein shake without the protein. You have the tools to read your Bible for yourself, to self-feed on the feast that is Scripture. It is crucial for personal and corporate revival.

One thing that helps us at Love Church is the accountability of being in a small group. Currently, I am in a group with a wide variety of men, and we meet in the early morning on Fridays. We have a group leader who facilitates a discussion of what we read on our own the past week. Each man picks a day of the week to share three to five minutes of what the Lord spoke to him. This puts some basic accountability and incentive on each man to stay in the Scriptures every day. We have non-believers, new believers, and mature believers in our group, and I love hearing from each of them!

Third Ingredient: Response

Hebrews 4:12 says, "For the word of God is alive and powerful. It is sharper than the sharpest two-edged sword, cutting between soul and spirit, between joint and marrow. It exposes our innermost thoughts and desires." When you recover the Word of God and read it, it dices you up! It's like spiritual surgery. When God's law was recovered in the temple in Josiah's day, he tore his clothes in grief that it had been lost for so long. He was like Hulk Hogan when he ripped up his bright yellow shirt before each match!

You need to allow God's Word to have a similar effect in your life. However, your response can't stop with just emotion. It must also lead to action. You must apply God's Word to your life to experience its best blessings. Hulk Hogan wouldn't just get emotional and rip off his shirt; he would act and beat up the enemy!

God promises restoration in your heart if you respond to His Word and obey it. When your life is committed to Jesus and you are growing and being sanctified in Him, you are more effective as an agent for change in your church, your community, and the world.

My prayer is that this would be your primary

motivation for self-feeding on Scripture: to see God change your life and the lives of those around you. It's possible, and you can start right now!

About the Author

Pastor Todd Doxzon is the founding pastor of Love Church. He has been married to his wife, Denise, for twenty years and has twin sons, Tzion and Blaze, who are eighteen years old. His call is to help as many people on the planet as possible to become self-feeders.

About Sermon To Book

SermonToBook.com began with a simple belief: that sermons should be touching lives, *not* collecting dust. That's why we turn sermons into high-quality books that are accessible to people all over the globe.

Turning your sermon series into a book exposes more people to God's Word, better equips you for counseling, accelerates future sermon prep, adds credibility to your ministry, and even helps make ends meet during tight times.

John 21:25 tells us that the world itself couldn't contain the books that would be written about the work of Jesus Christ. Our mission is to try anyway. Because in heaven, there will no longer be a need for sermons or books. Our time is now.

If God so leads you, we'd love to work with you on your sermon or sermon series.

Visit www.sermontobook.com to learn more.

REFERENCES

Notes

[1] Strong, James. "G4704: spoudazō." *A Dictionary of the Words in the Greek Testament and the Hebrew Bible*. Faithlife, 2009.

[2] "US National Debt." US Debt Clock. https://www.us debtclock.org/.

[3] "Abortion Statistics: United States Data and Trends." National Right to Life. https://nrlc.org/uploads/factsheets/ FS01AbortionintheUS.pdf.

[4] Leahy, Michael. "Appendix A." In *Porn @ Work*. Moody, 2009.

[5] *Merriam-Webster Dictionary*, "exegesis." https:// www.merriam-webster.com/dictionary/exegesis.

[6] *Merriam-Webster Dictionary*, "eisegesis." https:// www.merriam-webster.com/dictionary/eisegesis.

[7] *Encyclopaedia Britannica*, "Babylonian Captivity." https:// www.britannica.com/event/Babylonian-Captivity.